PICTURE A COUNTRY

Jamaica

Henry Pluckrose

W
FRANKLIN WATTS
NEW YORK • LONDON • SYDNEY

This is the Jamaican flag.

First published in 1998 by
Franklin Watts
96 Leonard Street
London
EC2A 4RH

Franklin Watts Australia
14 Mars Road
Lane Cove
NSW 2066

Copyright © Franklin Watts 1998

ISBN 0 7496 3021 3

Dewey Decimal Classification Number

A CIP catalogue record for this book is available from
the British Library

Series editor: Rachel Cooke
Series designer: Kirstie Billingham
Picture research: Juliet Duff

Printed in Great Britain

Photographic acknowledgements:

Cover: James Davis Travel Photography t, Images Colour
Library br, Eye Ubiquitous bl (David Cumming)

AA Photo Library pp. 8, 11b, 24, 25t;
Allsport p. 25b;
Axiom Photographic Agency p. 27 (Ian Cumming);
Anthony Blake Photo Library p. 23t;
Stephani Colasanti p. 12;
James Davis Travel Photography p. 17;
Eye Ubiquitous pp. 16, 20, 22 &, 26 (David Cumming),
19 (Gavin Wickham);
FLPA p. 29l;
Getty Images p. 10 (Jon Gray);
Robert Harding Picture Library p. 29r;
John and Penny Hubley p. 21;
Images Colour Library pp. 13, 14, 15;
Frank Spooner Pictures p. 9;
Topham Picture Point p. 11t;
Trip p. 28 (L. Gullachsen);
Tropix Photographic Library p. 18 (M. Fleetwood).

All other photography Steve Shott.
Map by Julian Baker.

Contents

Where is Jamaica?

This is a map of Jamaica. Jamaica is a small West Indian island. The West Indies are a group of islands in the Caribbean Sea, which lies between North and South America.

Here is some Jamaican money. It is counted in dollars.

CARIBBEAN SEA

St Ann's Bay

Ocho Rios

JAMAICA

Port Antonio

Blue
Mountains

Spanish Town

Kingston

NORTH
AMERICA

SOUTH
AMERICA

Children First!

JAMAICA

$10

150th Anniversary of East Indians
Jamaica

JAMAICA

$2.50

150 th Anniversary of East Indians
Arrival in Jamaica

These are some
Jamaican stamps.

The Jamaican landscape

Some of the Blue Mountains are over 2000 metres high.
Their lower slopes are covered in trees and bushes.

Jamaica is an island of hills and
small rivers, with the high
Blue Mountains in the east.

A hurricane in Jamaica blew these empty
aeroplanes from an airport into trees.

The weather is hot throughout the year.
From August to October, the winds
can be very fierce.
These winds are called hurricanes.

The Jamaican people

Over two and half million people
live in Jamaica.
Most Jamaicans are black Africans.
They are descended from people who were
captured in Africa and sold in Jamaica
to work as slaves. Nobody is a slave in
Jamaica today.

People stop to buy fruit at this market in Montego Bay.

People from Europe, China and the Indian sub-continent also came to live in Jamaica.

Christopher Columbus was the first European to sail across the Atlantic to Jamaica. He landed there on 4th May 1494. This statue of him is in St Ann's Bay.

Where they live

Half of the people on Jamaica
live in towns.

This is the town hall in Negril.

The most important towns are Kingston,
Montego Bay, Negril, Ocho Rios,
Port Antonio and Spanish Town.

Devon House in Kingston was built in 1881 by George Stiebel, Jamaica's first black millionaire. It is now a museum.

The capital city

This old boat is tied up in Kingston harbour. Behind it lie the modern city's skyscrapers.

Kingston is the capital of Jamaica. Over 800,000 people live there.

Kingston is also the main port of Jamaica.

14

Many people go to Kingston to look for work,
so the city is growing bigger and bigger.

Mining in Jamaica

Bauxite is quarried in Jamaica.
It contains a metal called aluminium.
Aluminium is very light in weight.

Bauxite is grainy and earthy, like clay. It is dug up from just under the surface of the ground.

The bauxite is taken by ship to other places around the world where the aluminium is extracted from it.

Aluminium is used in electrical goods, for making tins, cans and saucepans, in aircraft and cars, and even for cooking foil and the tops of yogurt pots!

Farming

This Jamaican farm worker is harvesting pineapples.

Jamaican farmers grow bananas,
coconuts, pineapples, coffee, cotton
and the cane which gives us sugar.

Bananas hang in huge bunches, which grow up towards the sun. They are picked while they are still green.

Family life

This Jamaican family lives in Kingston.
Like many people in Jamaica,
the parents work very hard
to earn a living.

How does this Jamaican classroom look different from your own? How does it look the same?

Children in Jamaica have go to school until they are 12 years old, but over half stay on at school until they are about 17.

Jamaican food

This man is cooking spicy chicken on a barbecue to sell to passers-by.

Jamaicans enjoy spicy foods. Meat is often cooked on an open fire or barbecue and flavoured with pimento. Pimento is the fruit of a Jamaican tree. It is also called "allspice" because it combines lots of spicy flavours.

Other Jamaican foods include bammy (a kind of bread), rice and red beans, and lots of fruit and vegetables.

Fried red snapper is a favourite dish.

Here are some Jamaican fruit and vegetables: yam, sweet potatoes, akee, coconut, pineapple and green bananas.

Sport

Jamaicans enjoy sports of all kinds - athletics, fishing, golf, horse riding, sailing, scuba diving and tennis. The most popular game is cricket.

Jamaicans start to play cricket when they are very young. The best cricketers play for the famous West Indies team.

For tourists visiting Jamaica, scuba diving is a popular sport.

In athletics, Jamaican runners are among the fastest sprinters in the world.

Music and festivals

Many Jamaicans are Christians. Christmas and Easter are times of celebration with street parties and parades. People dance to reggae and other pop music.

This is a statue of Bob Marley (1944-1981), a famous reggae musician. Like some other Jamaicans, he was a Rastafarian (a Rasta).

Visiting Jamaica

Millions of tourists visit Jamaica each year.
Some come to enjoy its warm sea and
sandy beaches.

Tourists take boats up Jamaica's rivers to see the rainforests and the wildlife.

Some come to explore the island's beautiful rainforests, hills and mountains. Others come to search for lost treasure because many pirates used to live on Jamaica!

Index

About this book

The last decade of the 20th century has been marked by an explosion in communications technology. The effect of this revolution upon the young child should not be underestimated. The television set brings a cascade of ever-changing images from around the world into the home, but the information presented is only on the screen for a few moments before the programme moves on to consider some other issue.

Instant pictures, instant information do not easily satisfy young children's emotional and intellectual needs. Young children take time to assimilate knowledge, to relate what they already know to ideas and information which are new.

The books in this series seek to provide snapshots of everyday life in countries in different parts of the world. The images have been selected to encourage the young reader to look, to question, to talk. Unlike the TV picture, each page can be studied for as long as is necessary and subsequently returned to as a point of reference. For example, a Jamaican school might be compared with their own; a discussion might develop about the ways in which food is prepared and eaten in a country whose culture and customs are different from their own.

The comparison of similarity and difference is the recurring theme in each of the titles in this series. People in different lands are superficially different. Where they live (the climate and terrain) obviously shapes the sort of houses that are built, but people across the world need shelter; coins may look different, but in each country people use money.

At a time when the world seems to be shrinking, it is important for children to be given the opportunity to focus upon those things which are common to all the peoples of the world. By exploring the themes touched upon in the book, children will begin to appreciate that there are strands in the everyday life of human beings which are universal.